A SETTING OF SILVER

A SETTING OF SILVER

JEAN VAUGHN

Scythe Publications, Inc.
A Division of Winston-Derek Publishers Group, Inc.

PUBLISHED BY SCYTHE PUBLICATIONS, INC.
A Division of Winston-Derek Publishers Group, Inc.
Nashville, Tennessee 37205

Library of Congress Catalog Card No: 94-60945
ISBN: 1-55523-718-5

Printed in the United States of America

FOR LIZ,
BECAUSE SHE ASKED

A WORD FITLY SPOKEN
IS LIKE APPLES OF GOLD
IN A SETTING OF SILVER.

—PROVERBS 25:11

CONTENTS

INCLINE YOUR EAR

I WILL INCLINE MY EAR TO A PARABLE;
I WILL DISCLOSE MY RIDDLE UPON THE HARP.
—PSALM 49:4

It happened late one spring afternoon, during a time of year when kings normally go out to battle. But this year was different—the king had chosen to stay home. As he was walking upon the flat roof of his palace, he looked down upon the roof of one of his neighbor's houses. There, a beautiful woman was bathing herself. The king was filled with desire, and he coveted his neighbor's wife.

We all know the rest of the story—how David and Bathsheba committed the adultery that resulted in Bathsheba's pregnancy, and how David plotted to bring her husband, Uriah, home from the war to sleep with his wife. When this plan failed, David arranged to have Uriah killed, and then he married Bathsheba.

After David's son was born, God sent the prophet Nathan to rebuke David. No doubt Nathan must have wondered how to approach David. "How will I get him to listen? After all, if I anger him, he has the power to have me killed. Perhaps I can share the truth through a tale."

Thousands of years later, Tennyson confirmed this storytelling technique when he wrote the following: "Where truth is closest words shall fail,/When truth embodied in a tale/May enter in at lowly doors" (from "In Memorium").

Everybody likes a good story. Few people can resist the opportunity to hear one. If we say, "Let me tell you a story," people are all ears. We have their undivided attention. On the other hand, if we say, "Let me explain my theory of that," most people do not want to listen. Indeed, we may be numbed by a dull speaker who is delivering a dry speech, but we perk up at the mere mention of a story.

It's easier to understand what people are trying to say when they use ordinary life experiences to illustrate their point. And when we make the connection between a story and our own lives, the experience is even more powerful. Sometimes we have to be helped along in making the connection, but that doesn't diminish its power. When it sinks in, that's when we understand.

Stories that help people understand higher truths or help them see their own shortcomings are called parables. Parables have been defined in various ways, but they all have one thing in common. They place two events, or two things, side by side so that we can see how they are alike. Another popular definition of the parable describes it as "an earthly story with a heavenly meaning." But a parable is more than just a story. It comes from the Greek word *parabole,* which means a proverb, a comparison, or a symbol. And the Hebrew word *mashal,* which is used in the Old Testament, refers more to a proverb or comparison than to a story. In fact, *mashal* is usually a succinct, one-line proverb, such as "Every way of a man is right in his own eyes, but the Lord weighs the heart" (Proverbs 21:2).

A parable is also not the same as a fable or an allegory, although they do have similarities. Like parables, fables are stories that have meanings beyond their words. However, they often utilize animals and inanimate objects, rather than people, as their main characters. They end with a moral that usually points out the consequences of bad decisions or behavior.

Allegories, like parables, use stories of natural events and teach by comparison, but the characters and events become deeper symbols that are explained as the story develops. Jesus used this kind of comparison in his parable of the seeds and the soils (Matthew 13:1-9 and 18-23); the seeds and the soils become symbols for the sharing and understanding of the good news.

What, then, is a parable? Although it encompasses some elements of proverbs, fables, and allegories, it has perhaps a broader scope than any of the three. Webster's New World Dictionary, Third College Edition, says it is "a short, simple story, usually of an occurrence of a familiar kind, from which a moral or religious lesson may be drawn." By this definition, the entire Book of Job in the Old Testament may be a parable. And what about the beginning of chapter 17 of the Book of Ezekiel, which refers to the parable of the eagles and the vine? Another biblical parable can be found in the fifth chapter of Isaiah. Verses 1-2 describe this passage as a love song, but verses 3-7 argue that it is a story that teaches a spiritual truth.

However we attempt to define the parable, it's usually difficult to put in our own words. Perhaps that's why we hear it described so often as an earthly story with a heavenly meaning. One of my favorite definitions is one used by P.G. Wodehouse: a parable is a story that initially sounds pleasant, but it keeps something up its sleeve that, when revealed, knocks you flat!

God used the parable when he sent his prophet Nathan to visit King David (II Sam. 12:1-15). David had committed adultery with Bathsheba and arranged her husband's death so that he could marry her. But David would hardly have listened if Nathan had simply blurted, "God says you have sinned." No doubt David would have defended himself and denied any wrongdoing: "I am the King; Uriah was killed in battle, not by me." David would surely have dismissed Nathan rather quickly. But God instead chose to send Nathan with a parable: "There was a rich man and a poor man. The rich man had many sheep, but the poor man had only one little lamb that he had hand fed and loved like one of the family, a pet."

David listened. He saw the sin of the rich man when he refrained from using one of his own flock for a visitor's dinner and instead took the lamb of the poor man to serve for dinner. David was furious and called down judgment upon the rich man. It was not until Nathan pointed out to David that he himself was that man that David made the connection: "I, a rich man, have many wives, but I took the only wife of Uriah."

The literature of the world, particularly the Bible, is rich in its use of parables to teach valuable lessons. Isaiah 5:1-7, often called the Song of the Vineyard, compares the vineyard to the house of Israel. In Ezekiel 17:1-21, the word of the Lord came to Ezekiel, and he delivered an allegory comparing eagles to the house of Israel.

Perhaps the writer of Proverbs had parables in mind when he wrote, "A word fitly spoken is like apples of gold in a setting of silver" (Proverbs 25:11). In this proverb, the parable is the perfect setting for apt words and good teachings.

The greatest speaker of parables was quite possibly Jesus. Indeed, our thoughts turn to Jesus at the mention of the word "parable." He was not the first to use parables as a teaching tool, but he certainly perfected the technique. He used the word pictures of parables to fix permanently in his listeners' minds the truths about the Kingdom of God and God's grace.

Many of Jesus' parables were probably never written down. In fact, John said it would take many more books to record all Jesus said or did. However, we still have over forty of Jesus' parabolic teachings available to us in the Bible. And although many of Jesus' sayings are short metaphors or similes, they still have much of the teaching power of his parables.

One important aspect of parables that I'd like to mention is that the speaker of a parable always shows a loving respect for the listener's way of life, labor, and love. Jesus displayed this respect through his use of the common ways of the people among whom he dwelt to teach them about himself and his Father. His parables helped them to understand what he was teaching because he used terms and situations that they could relate to.

My own use of the parable as a counseling tool grew out of my experience in the Education for Ministry program called "theological reflection." Education for Ministry is a four-year extension class from the University of the South in Sewanee, Tennessee. The class is designed to help lay people equip themselves for their own ministries.

Theological reflection involves examining an ordinary event in one of the participant's lives so that all members of the class can learn from it. The process begins when one person relates an event. The other class members solicit his or her thoughts and feelings about the event, then they all share any thoughts and feelings that they have had about similar events in their own lives. The next step is to develop a metaphor that captures those thoughts and feelings. The class deals with the metaphor and its meanings culturally, traditionally, biblically, and so on. For example, what would it be like to live in the world of that metaphor? What's right? What's wrong? What in the Bible supports or contradicts it? Then the class discusses what they learned.

After four years of dealing with theological reflection, it became easier to think in those terms when working through even the smallest problem. It seemed natural to ask the people I counseled to share their thoughts and feelings and to create metaphors to describe their problems.

When using one of Jesus' parables to support a metaphor, the idea occurred to me that perhaps people could write and share their own parables. In one of my counseling sessions, when there was a breakdown in communication between parents and their son, we needed something to get the son's attention. The result was "The Parable of the Long Horns," which you will read about in the next chapter.

The successful use of the parable in that counseling session was the catalyst for many more parables to follow. Most have had phenomenal results. A few have failed—not because the technique is at fault, but because the parable was either not well developed or not well conveyed. Needless to say, the counselor as well as the counselee learned a lot along the way.

Parables don't fit into every counseling situation, but they are quite valuable in those cases in which there has been a breakdown in communication. Topping everyone's list of what's important in relationships is likely to be communication. This is true among friends, peers, generations, and between spouses, lovers, employers and employees, and on and on. Communication is so important that we attend classes, workshops, seminars, and lectures and read books to find out how to do it better.

Misunderstandings make communication so difficult sometimes. We *hear* something differently than how it is *said*. And sometimes what we *say* is not what we *mean*. We have all experienced such misunderstandings. "But I thought you said…" "No, I didn't say that!" "What I meant was…" Then you try to figure out what really caused the misunderstanding in the first place. Unfortunately, many times we never have the opportunity to clear it up, and we go our way believing something that is not really true.

Misinterpretation is another pitfall in communicating. Case in point: last winter I made a pot of turkey stew (my husband and I are limiting fat and cholesterol). The next day, I served the leftovers with a sandwich for lunch. I also had a leftover bowl of turkey and rice soup and thought it would be a good idea to mix the two. But since I knew my husband wasn't too fond of turkey and rice soup, I served him the plain stew and ate the mixed stew myself.

He said to me, "You have rice and I don't."

I *thought* he meant this in a teasing way, but I've misinterpreted such things in the past, so I decided to check it out. "Do you want some rice in yours?"

He replied, "It's fine the way it is."

I was more uncertain than ever. I *thought* he was teasing and *might* be saying, "I really would have liked some rice to jazz this up, but since you didn't put any rice in it, I'll eat it just the way it is. You can put some rice in it if I have to eat it again tomorrow."

But I still thought I ought to check it out again. "Do you want me to mix some rice soup in with yours next time?"

"No, I don't want rice in mine."

Now *that* I understood. I couldn't misinterpret it, because he shook his head slowly and smiled. The message here is clear: in communicating with other people, we have to be aware of voice tone and body language, too.

Communication can break down for a variety of reasons. For instance, we may feel foolish for thinking something is a problem and try to put it out of our minds, but it often creeps back to haunt us. Then we send false messages to someone who misinterprets them, and we find ourselves in a vicious circle of miscommunication.

At other times, communication breaks down because we are too shy about a subject, or unsure, or afraid we will hurt someone's feelings or be misunderstood. And sometimes communication fails because the other person with whom we want to communicate won't listen, or they change the subject, belittle us, or tell us we are imagining things.

When there are barriers to communication, real or imagined, a parable can help. A parable can't be used to solve every problem, but it can be immensely helpful in sharing one's feelings while maintaining respect, patience, and love between two people or groups.

Aggression never helps anyone establish a loving, caring, or respectful relationship. It only proves who has the most power and control. A parable helps one say humbly and gently, "I have these feelings. Please help me to work through this problem." A parable doesn't accuse or threaten or attack. It doesn't put the listener on the defensive.

A parable is patient. It doesn't say "You have to stop or start something *now!*" It says, "Let's see if we can fix this together. Let's bear with one another in love."

7

We all sin and we all fail, particularly in our relationships. It's much better to bear with others in love than to attack them or to suffer silently and carry a grudge. Parables help us to forgive, and since they help us focus on ourselves instead of the other person, parables teach us not to blame each other.

In Ephesians 4:2-3, Paul said to "be completely humble and gentle; be patient, bearing with one another in love. Make every effort to keep the unity of the Spirit through the bond of peace." Holding a grudge, gossiping about each other, avoiding contact, giving each other the "silent treatment," and exchanging sharp and bitter words—all these break down the bond of peace. A parable can be the peacemaker that opens the way for meaningful communication.

The person telling the parable has time to present his or her viewpoint in a non-threatening manner without the listener becoming defensive. Telling a story often makes it easier to say the things that they have been unable to say before, and it prevents blame and encourages communication so that everyone can work out their problems. People can use parables to get beyond anger, animosity, and hurt feelings to the loving things they really want to say.

THE PARABLE OF THE LONG HORNS

Tom and Ellen looked at each other helplessly and then at me expectantly. I hadn't seen them in a counseling session since their son Jason had been a senior in high school two or three years ago. At that time they had literally pulled him through graduation by his boot straps. Neither one said anything, so I started a conversation I hoped might be neutral. Soon their story came tumbling out.

Jason had dropped out of college and as far as they knew wasn't working. But he seemed to have money, and he stayed out all night and came back home occasionally to sleep or to have a quick meal. He was distant and surly, and he became angry and left the house if they questioned him in any way. They had smelled alcohol on his breath and guessed from his behavior that he was using some kind of illegal drug. He had lost weight and didn't seem to care about his appearance.

I asked them to describe their thoughts and feelings about Jason's life right now. How did it feel when Jason behaved this way? What were their thoughts about it? Could they describe what it was like in terms of a metaphor? Was there an incident or parable in the

Bible that captured the same thoughts and feelings as the metaphor?

We soon discovered that they felt like the poor man named Lazarus who went to be with Abraham. To them, Jason was like the rich man who went to Hades. He was calling out to them, but they were separated from him by a deep pit like the one between the rich man and the poor man in Jesus' parable in Luke 16:19-31. "It's like being separated by a wide gulf," they said.

"Maybe we can write a parable for you to share with Jason," I suggested to them. "It's been my experience that people will listen to a story if you choose the right time."

They agreed, and we spent the next two sessions composing and rehearsing the parable. Tom and Ellen waited for a time when Jason joined them for a meal and asked him if they could share with him a short story they had composed. Jason didn't know it then, but when he perked up his ears and agreed to listen, he was going to get zapped with a tale so powerful it was going to change his life!

Tom and Ellen took turns telling this parable just as they had rehearsed it: "There was once a tribe of people who lived in a valley of great beauty. Living in this same valley was a herd of wild cattle with long and dangerous horns. The people wanted to stay in their beautiful valley, but they feared for their safety, especially that of their children. So they constructed a large corral with a high, strong fence and herded the cattle into it. Occasionally they would find a stray bull and attempt to put him in the corral with the others, but this was very difficult, and they often let out two while trying to put in one. So they dug a deep, wide pit in front of the gate and covered it over with a cattle guard. This way, they could haul in the strays in a truck, back over the cattle guard, and deposit them in the enclosure without the other cattle crossing the guard to come out.

"The children of this tribe began to go to the corral and stand on the cattle guard and tease the cattle. Some children even began to go into the corral and pull the tails of the cattle and entice them to chase them. The children would then rush back over the cattle guard and be pulled to safety by their waiting parents.

"One day a storm came, and a great flood of water rushed down through the beautiful valley, dug a deep ditch that ran through the pit, and washed away the cattle guard. Soon the people discovered that some of the children were stranded in the corral with the dangerous cattle. The children cried out to them, but the pit was too deep for the parents to cross. They tried to throw weapons to the children so they could defend themselves, but the ditch was too wide. They did not know what to do.

"We are those parents, Jason. We want to help you get away from the danger that is destroying you, but we don't know how to reach you."

Tom and Ellen later told me that Jason began to cry. Their parable had built the bridge between them and Jason and had prepared him to accept the services of an alcohol and drug abuse program.

THE PARABLE OF THE
GOLDEN DOOR KNOB

HERE I AM! I STAND AT THE DOOR AND KNOCK.
—REVELATION 3:20

Judith was the last person I expected to see sitting on the couch beside me in a counseling session. She and her husband Jonathan seemed to be two of those "salt of the earth" people. Their three small children were well behaved, and the whole family was active in church. Jon and Judith were both members of the diaconate and often filled other positions, like that of the worship leader or door greeter.

Judith began to apologize. "I know this doesn't seem like a very big problem, and I shouldn't even be taking your time, but..." Judith had heard me discuss parable writing in a group recently, and she wanted to compose one to see if it might help her in her situation with Jon.

It seemed to Judith than Jon was always ready to respond to everyone's needs except hers. If a call came from a friend, a co-worker, a neighbor, or even a slight acquaintance, Jon was ready to respond. He would even get up from the table and leave his supper to go help someone who, in Judith's opinion, could just as well have been served later. But when *she* asked for his time, Jonathan was always tired or busy with something that just had to be finished.

I asked Judith to share her thoughts and feelings about Jon not responding to her. "What's it like in terms of a metaphor? Is there an incident in the Bible that captures those thoughts and feelings?"

Judith said she felt like Jesus must feel when he stands at the door and knocks but no one answers. I suggested we might write a parable to help her convey those feelings to Jon. I warned her that even if she did compose a parable, her husband might not be a good listener unless she chose a time when he would not be likely to say he was tired or busy. "When do you and Jonathan do your best talking?" I asked.

"I guess it's at night after the kids are in bed and we work on the wood pictures. But I've already tried to use that time to tell him how I feel, and when we get anywhere near to a serious conversation about feelings, Jon says he can't talk and concentrate on the picture at the same time, and he has to get it done for "so and so" for a birthday present. So I just shut up and glue down the pieces where he puts them, and I talk about the kids or other things while he just says, 'Hmmm.'"

I winced. I had been the recipient of one of Jon's pictures made of small pieces of wood fitted together to make a magnificent old barn. Had Judith tried to share with Jon as she had helped him construct it?

Together we composed and rehearsed Judith's parable and decided that the time they spent together in the evenings on the pictures was probably still the best time for her to present it. All Jonathan would have to do was listen. And listen he did. Judith said later that halfway through the tale, Jon had laid down his coping saw and wooden slats, his glue bottle sat drying out, and he was looking at her like he had discovered for the first time that she was a person who needed him, too. This is the story Judith told him:

"You know, Jon, I heard about a man once who had a great and beautiful house high on a hill. This man was loved by all his family and friends. His coworkers and neighbors all respected him and asked for his advise and help.

14

"In his great and beautiful house high on a hill the man had a workroom where he kept so busy that he sometimes missed a call for his help, so he decided to install a great door with a door knob for each person who might desire to come in and ask for him, even if he was doing something as essential as eating supper. (This is where Jon put down his coping saw.) For his wife he installed a beautiful door knob made of pure gold.

"One day the wife needed the help of her husband. She went to the workroom door, took hold of the golden knob and turned it, but nothing happened. It would not open the door. She turned and turned it to no avail. She even pounded on the door, but the man was so tired and so busy that he did not hear her and never came.

"Jon, I feel like that wife. Everyone has access to your door except me. My door knob just turns around and around and never opens the latch."

A few weeks later, Jon brought me a beautiful companion picture for my old barn. "My greatest joy, now," he said, "is to tell someone, 'Sure, I'll change the brakes on your car, but it will have to be after Judith and I get back from taking the kids on a picnic.'"

THE PARABLE OF THE
BOWLING KING

WHEN PAUL CAME TO JERUSALEM, HE TRIED TO JOIN THE
DISCIPLES, BUT THEY WERE ALL AFRAID OF HIM,
NOT BELIEVING HE REALLY WAS A DISCIPLE.
—ACTS 9:26

Matt sat across the coffee table from me in the church parlor. We were both drinking the iced tea I had prepared and had exchanged a few pleasantries about our respective churches. He set his glass on a coaster and folded his arms and crossed his legs.

Uh-oh, I thought. He doesn't really want to tell me the whole story. I opened my arms and leaned toward him, hoping he would respond accordingly and open up.

"I know you're wondering why I called you," he began.

His silence indicated to me that he expected an answer, so I mumbled, "Yes." He rose from his chair, turned his back, and rubbed the back of his neck as he gazed out the window. When I didn't say anything else, he turned to me and said apologetically, "You're probably wondering why I didn't go to my own pastor." I smiled faintly and thought to myself that it was too bad he didn't know what he was thinking as well as he knew what I was thinking. But I decided that it was time to use my counseling techniques. I gestured to his chair and said, "Why don't you just sit down, Matt, and start at the beginning of your story, and you can tell me later why you're here."

He seemed relieved and immediately sat down and leaned forward. Now we were getting somewhere.

"The problem is between me and my pastor," he began. Matt told me he was the chair of the evangelism committee, and the gist of the problem between him and his pastor was that they seldom agreed on anything. According to Matt, the pastor often dictated what the evangelism committee should do and frequently changed or altered their plans. It didn't take long to figure out that Matt and his pastor were engaged in a power struggle.

We talked about his thoughts and feelings, then I asked him to create a metaphor to describe what it was like when his pastor derailed his evangelism plans and activities.

Matt didn't take long to answer. "It's like being run over with a steam roller," he said.

"That's got to be a pretty helpless feeling," I reflected, but I had a hard time visualizing Matt flat as a pancake. He was over six feet tall and a little hefty around the belt area.

"I don't feel as helpless as I feel mad," he corrected me.

"What are you doing to help solve the problem?" I asked.

"I'm telling him off. And he just stands there like he's shocked that I should be so upset just because he's helping me. And, somehow or other, we wind up doing things his way. I'm ready to resign or leave the church."

"Maybe the feeling is more like having cold water thrown in your face...kind of how Paul must have felt when he visited the apostles and tried to convince them of his new self."

"That's it exactly!" He seemed amazed that I had captured his feelings.

"I have an idea, Matt, that may keep you from throwing in the towel." Then I described the technique of using a parable to gain someone's attention and cooperation. We talked about Jesus' use of parables and how we could use his techniques as well.

Matt was all for it. He really didn't want to leave his committee or his church, and he sincerely liked his pastor in other aspects of his ministry. He also revealed that the pastor was "muscling in" on other committees and church leaders and attempting to "strong arm" them into doing things his way. They, too, were frustrated and angry and were talking about resigning or leaving the church.

After explaining to Matt the process of choosing the right time and the right subject to grab the listener's interest, we went to work. The place for him to talk with his pastor would have to be away from the church (pastor's turf), and the parable would be about bowling, since that was the pastor's favorite way to relax. Matt asked him to meet for a game at the bowling alley but told him to come thirty minutes early for a cup of coffee so that they could discuss something on Matt's mind.

Matt said he just jumped right in as soon as the coffee came because he was so anxious to share his parable. The pastor looked perplexed as Matt began his story:

"There was once a good and righteous king. He wanted his kingdom to be the best in the land. He wanted his subjects to be happy, prosperous, and the most successful in the land. The king noticed that they were outstanding in almost everything they did except bowling. The king was an expert bowler, so he decided to instruct his subjects so that they would be experts, too."

Matt said that this was where the pastor's look of perplexity changed to one of amusement. Apparently he thought Matt was going to share a joke with him. But whatever he thought, Matt continued, and the pastor was destined to get the revelation of his life.

"As each one came up to bowl, the king told him or her where to stand, how to stand, how to hold the ball, how to swing, where to look and aim, and when to turn loose of the ball. As the subjects tried to do it just like the king, each one became worse and worse, knocking down only a few pins or guttering the ball. In order to train them and let them know when they were bowling incorrectly, the king would throw a cup of ice water right into the subject's face. Then the king would take the ball and throw it for the subject and then enter his score.

"The subjects became very frustrated, and many gave up. There was much discontent in the kingdom, and some even talked about moving to another kingdom."

Matt later told me that his pastor stopped him at this point and asked, "You're talking about me and the church, aren't you?"

Matt said they talked for an hour and a half and never did bowl a game that day. He shared the rest of his parable with his pastor, explaining that the king finds out that all bowlers don't have to take the same stance, have the same swing, or use the same size ball to knock down all ten pins. But the pastor was well ahead of Matt and even improved on the parable that we had created. He said that the bowler doesn't have to bowl 300 to be successful! What a good way to end the parable, I thought.

It was weeks later when Matt called me again to report that things were going much smoother in his church. Matt and his pastor had been bowling the day before, and that's when the pastor had thanked him profusely for the way he had shared his concerns in a parable. In fact, the pastor even said he was now writing and using his own parables!

THE PARABLE OF THE FRAGILE BUTTERFLY

THEY WERE USING THIS QUESTION AS A TRAP IN ORDER
TO HAVE A BASIS FOR ACCUSING HIM.
—JOHN 8:6

I had just dropped off to sleep when my phone rang shortly after midnight. My slow "Hello?" was answered by a woman's voice. "This is Helen," she said. "I'm sorry to call you so late."

Why do people always apologize when they need help? I wondered to myself. My irritation came from being awakened as much as it came from having someone apologize. But I pulled myself together and asked, "What is it, Helen?"

Her story was just another chapter in a saga that had been going on for months. Her husband Bruce had not come home from work and was probably at a bar drinking. He usually made it home before midnight after a four- or five-hour drinking spree. If Helen questioned him, he became verbally abusive and lately had been threatening physical violence as well.

I knew enough about alcoholism to know I didn't know enough to counsel Helen, so I had referred her to Alanon. We kept in touch often by phone and occasionally through personal visits. I reinforced the things she was learning, especially about how to stop enabling Bruce to be an alcoholic. I also wanted to be sure the children were not suffering. So far, they hadn't been too involved in his late night appearances, but Helen had recently stopped making excuses for Bruce not coming home for supper two or three times a week. As is typical in similar situations, the children had thought it was their fault because they had done something wrong.

Before we had finished our conversation, Helen heard Bruce coming in and quickly hung up so that she could pretend she was asleep.

Now I was wide awake! An hour later, I was still awake and feeling very helpless and inadequate in responding to Helen's needs. It was only after I had vowed to do "something" that I was able to settle down and get back to sleep. I would call Helen and ask her to stop by after she dropped the kids off at school the next morning.

Helen had barely greeted me the next day when she began to cry. Bruce had been very angry when she had pretended to be asleep and had dragged her out of bed to verbally berate her about Alanon. If I thought *I* had felt helpless, Helen was completely bewildered. We both thought it was imperative that Helen call her Alanon counselor as soon as possible.

Before I knew it, I was slipping into the theological reflection model from my Education for Ministry class and was asking Helen to describe her thoughts and feelings during her encounter last night with Bruce. "In terms of a metaphor, what's it like to have those thoughts and feelings?" I asked her.

Helen and I each came up with a few metaphors, and I told her about a time in my life when I had had some of those same feelings. Finally, the light bulb came on, and Helen exclaimed, "It's like a Catch-22! If I nag him, it's wrong. If I try to be nice and cheery and act like everything is normal, it's wrong. If I ignore him, it's wrong. It's a Catch-22!"

Wow! I thought. How are we ever going to turn that into a parable? But I felt compelled to go forward. "Can you think of any situation in the Bible that was a Catch-22?" I asked.

Helen looked at me like I had lost my mind, but she was clutching at straws herself, so she decided to go along. We spent some time naming this situation and that one, but we couldn't think of anything that seemed just right.

Finally, I pulled out a reference book that had all the names of everyone in the Bible, and we began with the letter A. It was when we got to the letter J that we both looked at each other and said simultaneously, "Job!" But after we examined Job's story, we felt he was not in a real "Catch-22" situation. Job's story was more about faithfulness in adversity than about being punished no matter what he did. But the letter J did lead us to Jesus, and we recalled several incidents in which the Jewish leaders tried to put him in a Catch-22 position. Jesus, being wiser than his adversaries, always prevailed.

That reminded me of the story of the man who approached a wise man with a bird in his hands and asked, "Is it dead or alive?" If the wise man had told him the bird was dead, the trickster would turn the bird loose and let it fly away. If the wise man had said it was alive, the man would crush the bird and open his hand to show it dead. The wise man, being wiser than his opponent, instead replied, "You hold the answer in your hands."

I talked with Helen about the power of that story and the great truth to be learned from it. "Jesus used stories to illustrate the truths he wanted to convey to people," I added.

"You mean parables?" Helen asked. By now, she had briefly left behind her concern about Bruce, and I hated to bring her back to it. But I explained the process of creating and presenting a parable and suggested we write one for her to share with Bruce.

"I'll do anything," she vowed, so we began to examine Bruce's interests and think of times that would be appropriate for her to share her parable with him. She said that he spent most of his free time drinking and watching T.V. "But," she added, "he used to collect butterflies."

"Butterflies? Are you serious?"

"No good, huh?"

"Let's go for it," I suggested. By then, it was getting very close to lunchtime. Helen would have to pick up her kindergartner soon, so we had only a few minutes.

Helen suggested she get out some of Bruce's best specimens and display them on the T.V. Then when Bruce noticed them, she would tell her parable.

On the T.V.? Why not? It was better than her earlier suggestion of taping one to his beer can! (By this time we were a little giddy from laughter and anything seemed plausible.)

Helen followed through, and it was only four or five days later when Bruce casually asked, "How come you got out my old butterfly collection?"

The answer he got would profoundly affect him. Helen simply explained that she thought they were pretty, and then she said, "I'd like to tell you a butterfly story."

She told me later that Bruce's reaction was just his usual: not interested, not rejecting. So she began her story:

"There was once a woman..." Her parable was short, a plagiarism of the one I had related earlier, except the wise man was a woman, just an ordinary woman, and the bird was a butterfly. "I am like the woman," she told Bruce, "and my feelings are like the butterfly. When you come home late [we had decided not to mention his drinking], I don't know how to communicate with you. I used to nag, then I tried being nice and cheery. I tried being silent. I even tried to pretend I was asleep. My feelings are as fragile as that butterfly, and I don't know what to do to get you to open your hand instead of squeeze it."

Helen said she wasn't really crying, but tears were streaming down her face as she stood there in front of the silent television set and calmly finished her story. Helen confessed she was absolutely dumbfounded when Bruce fell to his knees, grabbed her around the legs, and began to sob. A week later she went with him to his first Alcoholics Anonymous meeting and heard him say, "Hello, my name is Bruce, and I'm an alcoholic."

Now there is no stopping that girl. The next lifesaving thing she wants to hear him say is, "I believe that Jesus is the Christ, the son of the living God, and I take him as my personal savior." But for now, she is content to take it one day at a time.

THE PARABLE OF THE MAGIC MOCCASINS

(IN LOVE) GOD PREDESTINED US TO BE ADOPTED
AS SONS AND DAUGHTERS THROUGH JESUS CHRIST.
—EPHESIANS 1:5

The tears began to well up even before Marilyn spoke. Her words came out in stutters: "I…it's V…V…Violet." I was sure something dreadful had happened to Violet. My imagination was going wild while Marilyn pulled herself together.

When she stopped sobbing, she explained her concern. Violet wanted to find out who her "real" parents were. Marilyn and Hank had adopted Violet when she was a few weeks old—a brown-eyed, brown-skinned beauty who was part Papago Indian and part Mexican American. Violet had just celebrated her thirteenth birthday and had revealed that the present she most wanted was to find her biological parents. Marilyn saw this as evidence that Violet loved her and Hank less because they weren't her "real" parents.

I couldn't resist sermonizing—no indirect counseling would suffice here. "Marilyn," I asked, "haven't you been reading any of the current literature on adoptees? Violet is only experiencing what thousands of other adopted children have already gone through and are still going through. According to what I've been reading, Violet's desire to know who she is is normal."

"There's more to it," Marilyn explained. "She's threatening to run away to Arizona. She says no one likes her. She went to the youth meeting at church once and said no one spoke to her. The other students at school won't be friends with her. She says it's because she is Indian and everyone else is white or black, and she wants to find her own people. I keep trying to tell her that we *are* her own people."

The tears came again, and all I could do was give her a tissue and put my arms around her. "W…w…would you t…talk to her?"

"Of course," I assured her, "if Violet is willing." I knew it wouldn't do any good to meet with a thirteen-year-old girl if she didn't want to. We set up an appointment for the next day, right after school. When I picked Violet up, I made a mental note of the mix of international students I saw filing out of Violet's middle school.

Violet greeted me eagerly. "My mother says you're going to help me."

"I'm going to try," I told Violet. But it was soon clear that what Violet regarded as "help" was not what her mother and I had in mind. She thought I was going to help her find the woman who gave birth to her. I hadn't the foggiest notion how to go about that, but I sensed that if I refused it would be "so long and goodbye." The only thing I could think of was to visit the genealogy department at the city library. Violet and I finished our coke session with plans to go there on Saturday morning. I called Marilyn to clue her in and to secure her indulgence.

We found out more about my Cherokee ancestors than we did about Violet's Papago ones, but that did let us form a relationship in which we could talk about Violet's thoughts and feelings. After a few sessions I suggested, "Why don't you write a parable that would let your parents know how you feel about this?"

"A parable? I thought those were the stories Jesus told."

"You're absolutely right, Violet. Jesus used the parable as a tool to help people understand a greater truth. You can do that, too.

Now, what truth about your thoughts and feelings do you want to share with your parents? Let's assign those thoughts and feelings a metaphor. What's it like being in your shoes?"

We decided that maybe it was like walking in someone else's moccasins and not knowing whose they were or where they were going. "I wonder if anyone in the Bible felt that way?" I asked.

We were surprised and delighted to find so many adopted people in the Bible, all the way from Moses and Esther to Paul's reference to believers being adopted into the family of God. We wondered how the gentiles had felt among the Jews. Then we read together some of Jesus' parables, and I shared a few of my own so that Violet would get the idea.

She went home to work on her own parable, and Marilyn called to say she didn't know what we had done, but Violet was already back to her old self. I couldn't resist saying, "You ain't seen nothing yet!"

Violet's parable was about an Indian princess (what else?), and she wanted to share it with Marilyn and Hank at one of our sessions. We practiced and set the date, keeping Marilyn and Hank guessing about the purpose of the meeting.

In Violet's parable, the Indian princess lost her moccasins and found a magical pair which gave her many wonderful experiences. But she still thought about her first pair. What if she had not lost them? Perhaps they were magic also. Where would she be now if she still had them? Would their magic have been as wonderful as the magic of her new pair? She longed to know and finally could no longer enjoy her magic moccasins.

I would have predicted Marilyn's tears, but Hank's reaction was a surprise. He jumped up and clapped his hands as if a light bulb had just come on in his head, like a cartoon character that gets a revelation. He began to tell us, before Violet had a chance, that Violet had been feeling just like the Indian princess. I felt it was important that Violet confirm her father's interpretation. I didn't think Marilyn was really convinced until Violet assured her that Hank was exactly right. Hank was so pleased with this new information that he began to make plans immediately.

Their research revealed that Violet's Indian mother had been killed in a car accident shortly after Violet's birth and that her father was unknown to anyone except her mother. Some of Violet's cousins live on the Papago Indian Reservation just outside Tucson, and Hank, Marilyn, and Violet visited them the the following summer. Violet even learned the Indian word for the flower whose name she shares.

After they came home from vacation, Violet wrote to one of her cousins, a girl about her own age, but she didn't receive an answer. When I asked Violet how she felt about that, her answer was typical of a fourteen-year old: "She's probably busy like me." Then she added thoughtfully, "Like me, she probably doesn't know what to say. We really live in two different worlds. Maybe someday I'll look her up again."

THE PARABLE OF THE DEVIOUS DRUG

"I think Jamie is on drugs," James blurted as soon as we had seated ourselves.

I tried my best Rogerian on him. "You've noticed some things that make you suspicious."

James told me everything. His son Jamie wasn't eating much at home. He was coming in very late or not at all, acting sullen and contrary, and accusing his parents of not trusting him. It sounded to me like James might be right.

I urged James to keep the communication lines open with his son, and we discussed some different ways to do that. James decided to ask Jamie to help him go get an antique truck he was buying for parts for another truck he was restoring. I warned James not to get into "drug talk," but to use the time just to communicate.

A week or so later, James phoned to say that Jamie and he had had a good time, and since then Jamie had been home for supper every night and was even kidding around with his younger sister. James was sure he had been wrong about the drugs and indicated we didn't need to see each other any more.

It was almost a month before James called me again. It was the same song, second verse, only this time he had caught Jamie smoking marijuana, and they had had a big confrontation. Jamie had told him that marijuana and some other drugs he called "soft drugs" were not addictive and wouldn't hurt him.

I told James a parable I had read somewhere about a boy who saw a beautiful mountain and decided to climb it. While he stood at the summit and felt like he was on top of the world, a rattlesnake appeared and convinced the boy that it would not bite him if he would carry it down the mountain to find a better place to live. The boy agreed to do so, but when he reached in his bag to take the rattlesnake out and deposit it in its new surroundings, the snake promptly bit him. When the boy asked the snake why it had bitten him, the snake replied, "You knew what I was when you picked me up. It's your fault when you die."

I wondered aloud if James might be able to help Jamie by telling him a similar parable. I explained the process of parable writing and described its use as a tool for communicating. James was eager to give it a try, and we began.

We examined his thoughts and feelings and looked for supporting evidence in scripture. James resisted creating his own metaphor, believing that my parable of the snake fit the situation exactly. He decided he would tell it to Jamie, except that he planned to use a scorpion, rather than a snake, as the animal character. "Jamie and I found a scorpion last summer at the lake cabin when we were moving some firewood," James explained.

I met with both James and his wife the next week, and they practiced telling their parable. They later shared it with Jamie, explaining to him that the scorpion was much like the marijuana. Both may try to convince you that they are innocuous, but in reality they are both devious and quite harmful.

After sharing their parable with their son, James and his wife soon entered a counseling program with Jamie at a hospital drug rehabilitation center. It wasn't until Jamie's high school graduation acknowledgment at church services about four months later that I was able to talk with Jamie.

"Dad told me you helped him write the story about the scorpion. Thanks." He gave me a big smile, and I received my reward.

THE PARABLE THAT
ALMOST FAILED

SETTLE MATTERS QUICKLY WITH YOUR ADVERSARY
WHO IS TAKING YOU TO COURT. DO IT WHILE YOU ARE STILL
WITH HIM OR HER ON THE WAY, OR HE OR SHE MAY HAND
YOU OVER TO THE OFFICER, AND YOU MAY BE THROWN INTO PRISON.
—MATTHEW 5:25

"You just tell him to leave you alone!" Carolyn advised Stephanie. Soon the other children were echoing Carolyn's words, but I could see that Stephanie didn't believe that would work. I didn't want the discussion to go any further, either, because Stephanie's father, Marten, was a deacon and a very active member of our church. If Stephanie revealed any more, these second graders would go home and tell their parents—and I dreaded what might happen to Stephanie. So I changed the subject and asked the children, "What might Derek do the next time Sean tries to pick a fight with him?"

We had been discussing the difference between comfortable and uncomfortable touch. Each child had shared examples, and we had focused on ways to say "no!" to those uncomfortable ones. Deep into the discussion, Stephanie had revealed that her father sometimes comes into her room and wakes her up at night by getting into bed with her and touching her.

It happens to one in four, I reminded myself. In this group of nine, it could be happening to another one, right here among people who are members of the church.

We closed our discussion, but I asked Stephanie to stay after class and help me clean up. I gently coaxed her to talk to me. "Tell me some more about the uncomfortable touch from your father, Stephanie," I said. "Then we will think of a way to help you."

In the short time we had together, Stephanie revealed that when her father comes into her room at night after everyone is asleep, he lies down beside her without any clothes on. The first few times this happened, he just hugged her and petted her, and it was nice. Then he asked her to take off her pajamas so that they could get closer. Recently, he had begun taking her shopping and buying her special treats and asking her to keep their secret so that her two younger siblings would not get jealous. When he began touching her private places and asking her to touch him, she decided she should talk to her mother about what had been happening. When Stephanie's mother confronted him, however, Marten said he had gotten up to go to the bathroom and just went in the wrong room. Stephanie got a scolding from her mother.

"Now," said Stephanie, "He comes back sometimes, but he won't touch me or let me touch him unless I say I will do it for a special treat and promise to keep our secret."

"Are you saying he promises you a special treat if you touch him or let him touch you?" I asked. I knew it was important that I get this right. Stephanie said yes and added that she felt uncomfortable with the arrangement. She also worried that her mother would find out and be angry with her for doing a bad thing. I tried to assure her that she had done nothing wrong and thanked her for telling me.

By then, Stephanie was ready to join her family in worship. As she headed out the door, she said, "See you next Sunday. I have to go now."

There's one consolation, I kept telling myself. At least she doesn't seem to be traumatized by this—yet. I spent the next day vacillating between confronting Stephanie's father before or after I reported Stephanie's situation to Child Protective Services. After much thought, I decided to do it before.

Matthew 15:18 tells us to go to a brother who has sinned and show him his fault. So I called Marten at work and asked him to meet me at church after he got off work so that we could talk about Stephanie. "Sure," he answered, and I started planning my strategy. I knew we weren't going to have time for small talk, and I didn't want him to walk out on me before I had said what I needed to. Telling a parable seemed appropriate even though I had only an hour to prepare.

Marten came into the church in a very pleasant and talkative mood. Apparently we were going to have our small talk after all. He exuded charm and authority, and I felt somewhat unprepared to do this delicately. I decided to take the assertive approach and be done with it. Finally, in his take-charge way, he asked, "What's this about Stephanie? Is she getting in trouble in Sunday School?"

"No, no," I assured him. "Other than being a little too quiet, she's doing just fine. But something she said on Sunday prompted me to share a story with you. Actually, it's a parable."

Marten spread his hands. "Okay, let's hear it."

"The story I want to share with you is about a man who raised oysters," I began.

Marten looked incredulous. "Oysters?" he repeated, raising his eyebrows.

"Stay with me," I pleaded. "You'll soon see how this fits in with Stephanie."

He shrugged his shoulders, and I continued. "In the course of his work, this man found three perfect pearls." Marten had three children, another daughter and son, both younger than Stephanie. I was hoping he would make the connection. "The first pearl he found was his favorite, and he placed it in a velvet box and decided to keep it for himself. The other two he gave away. One was made into a ring and graced the hand of a good and true man. The other was made into a necklace and was cherished by a beautiful woman. The longer these two people wore the pearls, the more lustrous they grew and the more lovely they became.

37

"The pearl in the velvet box, however, remained very dull, even though the man would open the box and gaze at it, sometimes touching it and taking pleasure in knowing he possessed it. Children are like pearls." I concluded. "They must be loved and shared in order to develop their luster. Children who are kept for one's own pleasure grow dull like the pearl in the velvet box."

When I paused, he rose and asked, "Is that it?"

I felt like a failure. I knew my parable was weak in places, and I realized my subtle references had not gotten through to him at all. Well, enough of the gentle approach, I thought. It's time to jump in with both feet. "Stephanie told me you have been coming to her bed at night and fondling her," I stated.

"*What?!* You are out of your mind, and you are certainly talking about something that's none of your business! You can't possibly believe everything a child says." By this time, he was standing over me, angry and loud. He then threatened to sue me if I ever talked to Stephanie or any other member of his family again.

As he turned to go, I said firmly, "I'm going to call Child Protective Services."

I sat there for what seemed like a long time and reflected on my parable. I should have explained that the ring and the necklace represented marriage for the two little pearls in the parable. I should have explained that Stephanie could have her whole life ruined by Marten's actions, just as if she were closed up in the dark box. Maybe I didn't think enough about his thoughts and feelings. I couldn't even recall if I had developed a metaphor. No wonder my parable had failed. Prayer seemed like a good idea, so I spent some time in that.

When I locked the church and walked out to the parking lot, I was surprised to see Marten sitting in his car staring into space. I stopped by his car, but he didn't even look up. Finally, I cautiously asked, "Marten, can I help?"

He began pounding the steering wheel, and I could see tears streaming down his face, but not a sound came from his lips.

Only the Lord got us through the next few days. Marten and his wife and Stephanie are all in therapy, and their prognosis is good. I never found out if Marten responded to my parable or to my threat to report him. Either way, I'll just praise the Lord that I was able to help.

THE PARABLE OF THE "MEANING WELL" QUEEN

IN YOUR HEART YOU PLAN A COURSE,
BUT THE LORD DETERMINES YOUR STEPS.
—PROVERBS 16:9

I could tell Jenny was very excited when she called me on the phone. We had barely exchanged hellos when she said, "I've written another parable, and I want to share it with you."

Less than an hour later, we were sitting in Jenny's sunny kitchen drinking herbal tea. Her enthusiasm was obvious, so I didn't waste any time in letting her get it out. "Tell me about your parable," I urged her. A few months ago, we had worked together on writing one for her husband. Later she had written one for her children, and both had been successful.

"This one is for my mother-in-law," she began. I saw a mischievous glint in her eye and wasn't too sure I wanted to hear this. Parables aren't for getting even with people, and I was afraid I was going to have to point out that fact.

"Have you shared it with her yet?" I asked tentatively.

"No, no. I wanted to share it with you first."

Thank goodness, I thought. "So, let's hear it," I told her. "Start with the problem and tell me how you processed it."

"Well, you know my mother-in-law moved here from Des Moines seven weeks ago." No, I didn't know that. But Jenny explained that her mother-in-law was a widow of eight years and was much older than her youngest child (Jenny's husband Dan). She had had an unsuccessful cataract operation, then a cornea transplant that was not much better, and her deteriorated eyesight had left her unable to drive. She was living with Dan and Jenny while they looked for suitable quarters near them so that they could provide transportation for her.

At first, Jenny continued, Mother Olsen had seemed a blessing. She loved to cook, and Jenny had been glad to share that responsibility. But Mother Olsen cooked only what Dan liked from his childhood—foods that were very buttery, very sugary. She always insisted on serving Dan first with things like the choicest piece of meat, or his favorite part of the homemade bread—both end pieces of crust at the same time.

The second part of the problem was that Dan's mother catered to his every whim, getting up when he came into the room to let him have the best chair, insisting they watch the television programs that Dan was interested in.

Jenny assured me she had tried talking to Dan, but he had brushed it off. He thought Jenny was overreacting and had misinterpreted his mother's behavior. After that, Jenny just didn't have the courage to talk to his mother. And the prospects of soon finding a place for Mother Olsen to live were not looking good. She was being very selective.

"Maybe you should write another parable for Dan," I suggested. I reminded her that he had been very receptive to the first one.

"I tried," Jenny told me, "but when I examined my thoughts and feelings, I realized they were all directed towards my mother-in-law. I really couldn't blame Dan for being treated like a king and for enjoying being mother's little boy again."

"Hold it!" I interjected. "What do you mean, you can't blame Dan? Did he take the chair Mom offered? Did he accept the choice pieces of food? Did he remind her that other members of the family also get to choose T.V. programs?"

Jenny looked at me pleadingly. "Let me finish. I think you'll be surprised."

I shrugged my shoulders and gestured for her to continue. She said, "I felt like Sarah must have felt when Hagar had a son by Abraham. Sarah just couldn't stand the competition and proceeded to drive Hagar away. That's just what I wanted to do with Dan's mother."

"I think I'm beginning to see how you feel," I told her. "But I'm not sure I have any more sympathy for Dan than I have for 'poor' Abraham."

"Wait until you hear my parable," said Jenny. Once again, I saw that mischievous glint in her eyes.

I told myself to shut up and said, "Now you have my curiosity piqued, so let's hear the rest of the story."

Jenny began, "Once in a far-off kingdom there lived a very happy family—a king, queen, princess, and prince."

I interrupted. "But you have two girls."

"Jean, you taught me yourself to disguise the characters."

I'd already forgotten to be quiet, so I clamped my hand over my mouth and raised my eyebrows to let her know she could proceed.

Jenny's parable told of a queen in a neighboring kingdom who was deposed and sought asylum with a royal family. She was so pleased to be with them that she catered to the king's every whim, much to his queen's consternation. Jenny described how the ruling queen felt when she couldn't handle that type of competition.

Jenny and I decided we had better do some heavy praying and ask the Lord to guide us step by step, because the last thing Jenny wanted was a misunderstanding among herself, Dan, and Mother Olsen. But what really happened in the telling of the parable bowled us both over.

She approached her mother-in-law with the idea that she, Jenny, needed some advice in regards to her relationship with Dan, and in order to explain the circumstances she wanted to share a story. Jenny said she never got to the part about how the king's wife felt about the other queen. Her mother-in-law interrupted her and said she just *knew* Dan was ripe for an affair with another woman and that they—she and Jenny—needed to nip that in the bud. What Dan needed was to learn to face up to his responsibilities and take care of himself. From that day on, they should both stop doing things for Dan and quit treating him like a king!

Jenny said her jaw dropped open, and she was speechless. I confess I was, too, when Jenny told me what happened. Three weeks later, Mother Olsen moved into a retirement center, telling Jenny that Dan would probably "come around" much better if he didn't have his mother around to help spoil him, too. She also said that Jenny should stand firm in their resolve not to cater to him!

I think that if I had a few clients like Mother Olsen, I would be out of business.

The Parable of the Forty Days and Forty Nights

My husband, Eldon, and I were fast approaching our fortieth wedding anniversary, and I wanted to do something special for this man who seemed to know instinctively what I have gone to countless university classes, seminars, and workshops to learn.

My first thought was to make out a list and title it "Forty Reasons Why I Love Eldon Vaughn." I had been intrigued with Joyce Landorf's tribute to her husband on their seventeenth anniversary, a similar composition titled "Seventeen Reasons Why I'm Glad I Married Dick Landorf."

I numbered one through forty and began. The first ten were fairly easy; I completed them at one sitting. But three days and several sittings later I was only up to sixteen. I elicited the help of our two daughters and finally got to nineteen. "You're always writing parables, Mom," they suggested. "Why don't you write a parable for Dad?"

"Why don't I?" I mused. I began immediately, but I made many false starts and dry runs. Those nineteen reasons continued to stare back at me, but I just couldn't come up with twenty-one more, no matter how hard I tried.

Forget the list, I told myself. Just concentrate on a parable. What are the steps? Oh, yes—thoughts and feelings. How do I feel when I can't come up with forty reasons why I love my husband? Frustrated, stupid, inadequate, and dumb. I wondered if Scheherazade ever felt that way when she was trying to think up a new story every day for one thousand and one nights.

Somehow or other the time began to waste away. I counted the days until our anniversary: forty-one. Well, if Scheherazade could bat a thousand, I could surely do forty, and I even had a head start—I already had nineteen story ideas. True, I didn't have her motivation, but I was determined.

The next evening as we retired, I announced to Eldon, "I have a story to tell you, and it has forty chapters. It's called 'Forty Reasons Why I Love Eldon Vaughn,' and I want to tell you one chapter each night."

"Sounds good to me," he agreed. "When do we start?"

"Is right now okay?"

"Shoot."

I began, "There was once a boy and a girl who were very much in love..." I described the way they had to see each other every day, the way their hearts began to beat faster and their palms grew damp when they saw each other. I told him that the girl practiced writing "Eldon loves Jean" or "Jean loves Eldon" and "Mrs. Eldon Vaughn."

Before long, Eldon was adding things like, "He thought she was the best thing since chocolate cake with chocolate icing." We both laughed at that, because I used to bake one almost every day for him when we were dating. (And then, quite suddenly, I knew I had number twenty on my list: He always eats my chocolate cake, even the time I forgot the soda.)

"Their love has grown over the years," I concluded. Then I ended my story with number one on my list: "He loves me more today than he did forty years ago."

The next evening I began with number two on my list, and before the story was over, Eldon had given me number twenty-one.

The next night it was the same. I felt as though I had discovered Scheherazade's secret: every night when she told a story, she got an idea for the next one.

And so it went until the fortieth night. We reflected on the forty years we had spent together, and Eldon finally asked, "Hey, what's the fortieth reason?"

"The fortieth reason why I love Eldon Vaughn is that he has given me thirty-nine reasons to love him!"

THE PARABLE OF THE LIFE JOURNEY

Piece of cake. That was my private thought as I heard Sally relay her concerns. The scenario sounded typical of a family caught up in a power struggle. The ten-year-old twins, Rachel and Rebecka, didn't want to come to Sunday School, worship, or Junior Youth Fellowship. Sundays had turned into Wardays. Sally, their mother, was so battle-fatigued that she sometimes gave in and let them stay home. Uh-oh, I thought. Intermittent reinforcement, the hardest to deal with. No matter—Adlerian Family Counseling would solve this one in short order. Piece of cake!

A month later we had dropped Adler and resorted to straight behavior modification: follow a behavior by a reinforcement, and that behavior will increase; remove the reinforcement for the unwanted behavior, and that behavior will decrease. It worked for a few weeks. If Rachel and Rebecka attended church activities with no complaints, they could earn a trip to their favorite restaurant. But now they were demanding bigger rewards. McDonald's just wasn't good enough. They wanted more. But of course they did; these kids weren't dummies.

Now Sally and her husband Dirk were sitting before me. "We're going to see about psychiatric therapy," they informed me. We had eliminated all possibilities of teacher and peer behavior that might be causing the twins' aversion to church. There didn't seem to be any. Observations in Sunday School and JYF indicated that the girls were happy once they attended. They just didn't want to take the first step. Was it something akin to school phobia? There was no evidence to support that. Moreover, we had let the twins choose casual clothes, thinking that maybe they didn't want to dress up. We had asked teachers not to make demands on them if they didn't volunteer. But they volunteered all the time! Dirk and Sally felt they had covered all the bases, including making threats and offering bribes.

I still felt that they were engaged in a power struggle and that perhaps the parents just weren't following through with our plans. "Are you willing to try one more thing before you resort to psychiatry?" I asked them. They admitted that they had already made the appointment, but it was still eleven days away, and they were willing to listen to my suggestion in the meantime.

"Let's write a parable," I told them. They looked at me like I had said, "Let's go have a cup of tea," as if that would solve their dilemma.

Soon we were examining their thoughts and feelings and attempting to express them in a metaphor. "What's it like to fear that your children are going to grow up agnostic or atheistic?" I told them the parable of the Ten Maidens, five of whom had no oil in their lamps to light the way for the bridegroom in Matthew 25. "Are you afraid your two little maids will be caught with their lamps empty when they face judgement?" I asked.

They were amazed at my correct guess. "That's exactly it!" they exclaimed, now eager to work with a metaphor. "It's like going on a trip, but when you get there and you open your suitcase, it's empty," they said.

Now that we had moved away from Rachel and Rebecka's behavior and were focusing on Sally and Dirk's feelings, they were excited. As we explored their metaphor and examined the girls' interests, Sally and Dirk said that playing with Barbie dolls was their daughters' favorite pastime. Thinking about my own grand-daughter's Barbie doll equipment, I asked, "Do their Barbies have an RV?"

Sally and Dirk wrote their parable using their daughters' Barbie dolls, clothes, and equipment. It went something like this: "There were once two sisters who decided to pack their suitcases, get into their recreational vehicle, and take a trip through life. When they got to the seashore, they unpacked their bathing suits, towels, umbrellas, and suntan lotion. They had a great time.

"Next they went to the mountains to do some skiing. They had all they needed: skis, poles, and warm clothes and boots. Again they enjoyed their visit very much.

"'Now, how about an ocean cruise?' suggested one. So they put their RV in storage and took aboard all their play clothes and party dresses. When they returned, they decided to go on safari, so they got into their RV and drove to the jungle. They looked especially beautiful in their khaki and camouflage clothes. In spite of the fact that an elephant chased them back into their RV, they had a wonderful time.

"Then they learned to bowl and play golf and had the cutest outfits to wear. They even went horseback riding and had jodhpurs and boots. They went dancing in frilly dresses and jogging in fancy little suits.

"As they neared the end of their trip through life, they decided they would like to go to Heaven. So they parked their RV at the gates to Heaven and opened their bags. But they found they had nothing suitable to wear to enter into the presence of God. They just hadn't prepared for this last stop!"

Sally and Dirk explained that they were afraid this would happen to their daughters, and they described how it made them sad that the girls might not be prepared. They loved them very much and wanted them to learn about Jesus and God and Heaven. Then they read to them Jesus' parable of the Ten Maidens and discussed it together.

The following Sunday, the family came into worship together wearing big smiles. Dirk gave me the "A-OK" sign, and Sally mouthed, "We cancelled the appointment!"

THE PARABLE OF
WHITE WATER CANYON

FOR GOD LOVED THE WORLD SO MUCH THAT HE GAVE
HIS ONLY SON, SO THAT EVERYONE WHO BELIEVES IN HIM
MAY HAVE ETERNAL LIFE. FOR GOD DID NOT SEND HIS SON
INTO THE WORLD TO BE ITS JUDGE, BUT TO BE ITS SAVIOR.
—JOHN 3:16-17

I didn't know the handsome young man I was having coffee with in my kitchen. I'll call him John Doe just because that's as generic as I can get.

John had explained to me on the phone the day before that he lived in a nearby town. His sister had been in a workshop I presented at a state-wide Christian Women's Fellowship retreat, and she had given him my card. He felt he couldn't go to his pastor, and he didn't want to meet me at my church. I could understand that. Lots of people don't want to come to church for a counseling session—someone might see them and get curious. I had come to the incorrect conclusion that he couldn't go to his pastor because they were in some kind of conflict.

"I'm gay!" he blurted out. I was glad I had swallowed my mouthful of hot coffee. When I didn't answer, he continued. "My pastor doesn't know."

"Is being gay a problem for you?" I asked. I know that sounds silly now, but that's what I said nevertheless. He told me that for him, being gay certainly was a problem and had been for eighteen of his thirty years of life. At age twelve when the other boys were beginning to notice girls, he began to notice the other boys. He tried to date in high school and became good friends with a few girls. But he never felt romantically towards any of them. Conversely, he developed no friendships with boys because he *did* have romantic feelings towards them. He excelled in his studies, track, and music. Since graduation from college, he had been teaching music in elementary schools. He was very good-looking—tall with curly black hair and a mustache. I had thought he reminded me of Tom Selleck the moment we met.

"I've been celibate since college," John explained, "because of AIDS, and…well, I've always felt it was wrong, a sin. What do you think?"

"I think you have probably chosen well in being celibate, John. In Matthew, Chapter 19, Jesus described some men who were eunuchs because they were born that way, some who had become eunuchs because they had been castrated, and some who chose to be eunuchs for the sake of the kingdom of God."

"No, no," he protested. "What do you think about homosexuality being a sin?"

I was still struggling with my own feelings about that, so I chose one of Jesus' tactics and answered with a question. "Why do you ask?"

Now we got down to the real problem. John had become friends with a young man who also taught in his building. They had been out together a few times, and he was either going to have to stop seeing him or go to bed with him. As the story unfolded, he began to cry. "I don't want to love men. I have prayed for six years for God to take this feeling away from me. Maybe there isn't a God, or maybe he has already condemned me because of my sin. Even my parents have condemned me and won't talk to me. My pastor would probably have me run out of the church if he knew. He has preached several sermons on the sins of Sodom and Sodomites and God's use of AIDS as their punishment."

"I hope you are wrong about your pastor running you out of the church," I said. "Many theologians are taking a new look at what the Bible says about homosexuality, because new research studies are showing that some homosexuals—like the eunuchs of Matthew 19:12—may have been born that way, some are made homosexual by others, and some choose to be for whatever their reason. I do know that God loves you and wants to help you."

I gave him the name of a Christian psychiatrist who works with homosexuals in therapy. I also encouraged him to talk with his pastor. We talked about John's thoughts and feelings about being gay and developed a metaphor. "It's like rafting down a rushing river with no oars, no rudder," he decided. "It really feels hopeless."

"What from the Bible supports or contradicts that metaphor?" I asked. He knew all the scriptures condemning homosexuality, but he knew very little of those that speak of hope, forgiveness, and grace. That Jesus died for him and loved him boggled his mind.

We read together several translations from Isaiah 56:3-8. "Isn't God saying that all people who love and honor him will not be forgotten?" I asked. "Aren't you classifying yourself a foreigner or stranger in the family of God?" Then I read verse 3 aloud again: "A foreigner who has joined the Lord's people should not say, 'The Lord will not let me worship with his people.'"

John continued to resist talking with his pastor because he was afraid his pastor would reject him. His excuse was, "Maybe he hasn't read Isaiah."

"We could write a parable for you to share with your pastor that would open the door for you to talk," I suggested, after explaining about parables.

Since he didn't know much about his pastor's interests, we would just have to go with what we had. Timing wouldn't be a problem. He could simply make an appointment and have his pastor's undivided attention.

Writing the parable was tougher. All we had was John's metaphor of a rudderless raft on a rushing river, so we developed

John's story from that. We never guessed the effect that John's parable of the "White Water Canyon" would have on his pastor. This was John's parable:

"There was once a young boy who frequently went rafting down the river in White Water Canyon. For a while his oars and rudder worked just fine. Then one day he discovered his oars were dysfunctional. So he threw them overboard and decided he could get by just fine with his rudder only. The river didn't seem too wild, and he coasted along in this manner for several years.

"One day when the boy had become a young man, he heard a man who was an authority on river rafting say that you shouldn't raft with only a rudder. Your raft would upset, and you would surely drown. This troubled the young man so much that he gave up rafting all together. The problem was that he still longed to go rafting down the river.

"Eventually he tried rafting without the rudder, but the raft went out of control, and he felt hopeless and lost. That raft is my sexuality, Pastor. The man of authority on rafting represents you and those who believe as you do."

John went on to describe how he had felt about his sexuality since age twelve. After he finished explaining his parable, they sat in silence for what John said seemed like ten minutes.

Finally the pastor spoke. "I'm on the same raft, John, and have been for years. My marriage is a sham. The only good thing to come from it are my daughters. I've tried preaching against homosexuality in the hope that that would make me heterosexual. I think you and I both should go into therapy with that psychiatrist."

How to Write
Your Own Parable

GREET ONE ANOTHER WITH A HOLY KISS.
—ROMANS 16:16A

I don't know what Paul meant by a "holy kiss," but I know it wasn't the kiss used by Judas in the Garden of Gethsemane. I've never heard about it or seen it done in my church, but many of us are good huggers. I asked around in some other denominations, and one woman said, "Oh, yes, we used to do that, but we don't anymore." When I pressed her to describe it, she said it was like a dry peck on the cheek. It sounded kind of like those kisses you see Europeans on television give when they hand out medals. No wonder they gave it up!

I think I know what a "holy hug" is. I've been in many board meetings and committee meetings where people squared off in opposite corners until someone finally said, "Let's pray about this." After prayer, these people usually meet in the middle of the room, sometimes in tears, and they hug each other in repentance and forgiveness. What's more, they'll greet each other next Sunday morning with the same kind of hug: "humble, gentle, and patient, with every effort to keep unity of the Spirit through the bond of peace" (Ephesians 4:2-3).

A "holy kiss" must surely be like that. I believe Paul was speaking figuratively and didn't really mean for us to just touch our lips to someone's face or hand, although that seems to have been an accepted greeting in first century Rome. I believe he wanted us to have an attitude toward others that is an expression of Christian love. When we greet each other, it should not be a routine, empty social greeting, but a greeting with the sincerity in which Christ greets us—holy! And when we share a parable that we have composed especially for someone, we greet them with a "holy kiss."

I have developed some steps to keep in mind when writing and planning parables. Although I have found this outline to be quite helpful, keep in mind that you don't have to follow it to the letter. Sometimes a step can be omitted, and sometimes the order of the steps can be changed.

Step 1—Define the problem/identify the concern. Our problems and concerns are not always easy to identify or define. (Remember Jenny's difficulty in defining her problem with her mother-in-law? At first, she thought her husband Dan was the source of the difficulty. But when she examined her thoughts and feelings more closely, she discovered that they were directed toward Mother Olsen instead.) When attempting to define what's bothering us, we often think that if someone else would just change something about *their* behavior, then our problem would be solved. The difficulty with that attitude is that we can't change other people— we can only change ourselves. So we must first take ownership of the problem. Once we admit the problem is our own, then we have the power to do something about it.

A good way to take ownership of a problem is to internalize it. Say to yourself, "I have strong feelings or react uncomfortably when this person does this." Make sure that you define the problem in behavioral terms. For example, don't simply describe someone as uncooperative or unhelpful. Instead, say something like, "I'm upset when this person makes the excuse of a prior commitment rather than helping me to clean the house." Remember that the problem is *your* unexpressed feelings and *your* inability to share successfully how that other person's behavior is affecting you.

Once you take ownership of the problem and define the behavior that is causing your uncomfortable feelings, then you are ready to write your parable and share it with that person. Keep in mind that in many cases the recipient of your parable will voluntarily modify his or her behavior to help eliminate the problem.

Step 2—Describe your thoughts and feelings about a problem or concern. Ask yourself the following questions: what were my thoughts when this problem occurred? How did it make me feel? It's often hard to realize that others don't *make* us feel the way we do. *We* make us feel the way we do. When we focus on ourselves, we take the spotlight off what someone else did or said and put it on our own reactions. If you are helping someone develop a parable, share with that person the times when you have had similar thoughts and feelings. If you are working on this alone, try to recall similar circumstances or situations in your life.

Step 3—Express those thoughts and feelings in a metaphor. Ask yourself what it's like in terms of a metaphor to have those thoughts and feelings. Try to think of a parallel experience that explains how you feel, and explore options until you really have one that captures your thoughts and feelings. This allows you to defuse the situation because you deal with the metaphor while the problem or concern is on the back burner.

Step 4—Examine incidents in the Bible that support or contradict the metaphor. Scripture becomes a meaningful resource in problem solving. Sometimes people never get around to writing the parable because God's word speaks to them in such a way that the healing process begins immediately and the parable is no longer necessary. Other times people change their metaphor when something they encounter in the Bible gives them a new perspective.

Step 5—Compose a parallel experience that expresses the metaphor and your thoughts and feelings about the problem or concern. "There was once a ..." seems to be a good way to start.

Writers and artists say that the first word or the first bit of color on the paper is often the hardest. You should try to use something in the story that will grab the hearer's interest. What does your listener like to do? What interests, hobbies, and issues are significant to that person?

People listen better to things they are interested in. Tell me you want to talk about football, and I may say okay just to be polite, but I probably won't listen very well. I will look you in the eye and smile and nod because I know those are good communication techniques, but I may be planning my grocery list.

Step 6—Share the parable with the other person. Whether you read the story or tell the story is up to you, but timing is of the greatest importance. You don't want to "cast your pearls before swine," so to speak. Remember that people don't like to be interrupted, and be sure to choose an opportune time. You may have to create a time like Helen did when she displayed the butterfly collection on the television set. Then just be patient. If you have chosen your setting well and say, "Let me share with you a story I wrote," they'll listen every time.

Sometimes the meaning of the parable is self-evident, and your listener will put two and two together for themselves—much like the Jewish leaders in Jesus' parable of the Tenants in the Vineyard (Mark 12:1-12). But sometimes you have to explain the parable, just as Jesus did when he explained the Parable of the Sower (Luke 8:11-15). In any event, always be ready with an explanation just in case the listener doesn't get it. Say, "I am that person…you are this person…this is the way I feel when…"

When you write your parable, keep these six steps in mind, but don't set them in concrete. If you choose to leave certain steps out, however, realize that your parable may not be fully developed, and you may not get the results you're after. I never explored my thoughts or feelings or developed a metaphor when I jumped in and wrote a parable to share with Marten about the man who raised oysters and found three perfect pearls. I didn't know anything about his interests or hobbies, but I did know he had three won-derful children. And when I finished telling the parable, I didn't even bother to explain it to him. But the important thing was that it helped me to admonish him (another of Paul's instructions to believers, in Colossians 3:16) humbly, gently, patiently, and in a bond of peace. I didn't blow it, but I came close—so close that I've never delivered another parable in that much haste.

In some circumstances, leaving out certain steps in writing your parable is permissible or even necessary. For instance, when help-ing other people, I always try to explore their thoughts and feelings. But in James' case, although he was able to discuss his thoughts and feelings about his son's drug problem, he resisted developing a metaphor. When we went on to Scripture, he pretty much resisted that, too. He wanted to get straight to work on writing his parable. The result was a story that was similar to the one I had shared with him about the poisonous snake, and it worked very well.

In another case, John Doe didn't know about his pastor's inter-ests, so we skipped that part of step four and just used John's inter-est in river rafting. And sometimes you have to change the order of the steps as you work through your parable. Very often, people can't come up with a metaphor until they have examined Scripture. Tom and Ellen, for instance, couldn't think of one until we looked at the story of Abraham and Lazarus.

However you work through this process, keep in mind Paul's words to the Colossians in Chapter 3, verses 12 through 14: "You are the people of God; he loved you and chose you for his own. So then, you must clothe yourselves with compassion, kindness, humility, gentleness, and patience. Be tolerant of one another and forgive one another whenever any of you has a complaint against someone else. You must forgive one another just as the Lord has forgiven you. Add to all these qualities love, which binds all things together in perfect unity."